Nature Explorers

Seashore

Nick Baker

An *Imprint of* HarperCollins*Publishers*

For my Dad. Many adventures were had on the beaches, cliffs, and mud flats of the Isle of
Wight in the United Kingdom. It was armed with shrimping net, mask, and snorkel that I had
my first real adventures.

ISBN: 978-0-00-720767-1
ISBN-10: 0-00-720767-0

NATURE EXPLORERS: SEASHORE.

www.harpercollins.com

ISBN: 978-0-06-089081-0 (in the United States)
ISBN-10: 0-06-089081-9

FIRST U.S. EDITION Published in 2007.
HarperCollins books may be purchased
for educational, business, or sales promotional use. For
information in the United States, please write to:
Special Markets Department, HarperCollins Publishers,
10 East 53rd Street, New York, NY 10022.

The name of the "Smithsonian," "Smithsonian
Institution," and the sunburst logo are registered
trademarks of the Smithsonian Institution.

Text © Nick Baker 2007
Photographer: Nikki English, except for those pictures credited on page 71
Flick book illustrations: Lizzie Harper
Colour reproduction by Dot Gradations Ltd, UK
Printed and bound by Printing Express, Hong Kong

10 09 08 07
7 6 5 4 3 2 1

Disclaimer: Many of the projects in this book involve tools, knives, fire, or cooking. All of these can be dangerous and require a good
deal of training and practice before they are safely used. Parents should supervise these activities and monitor the correct use of
tools until children can be considered competent to use them themselves. Do not drink any of the water you collect from these
habitats. In addition, common sense and basic precautions—knowing exactly where your children are and what they are doing at all
times, making sure they wear sunscreen and appropriate, protective clothing, and teaching them how to respect nature and safely
explore their surroundings—are the key to your children learning the joys of the great outdoors.

Contents

Flick the pages to see the crab move!

The seashore

Lots of good things happen in nature when one thing meets another. These can be times of the day—for example, at twilight and dawn when night meets the day—or times of the year, when spring transforms into summer. Or they can be physical things, such as where a beach merges into another habitat, like the ocean.

To naturalists, these times and places of transition are well known as they can concentrate periods of activity, making certain creatures easier to see. When spring finally arrives, we get a sudden rush of frenzied activity, birds sing, frogs spawn and flowers bud, and where one habitat blends into another, you often get a special kind of "edge"; a place that is inhabited by life from both places.

In this book, we explore the seashore, a habitat that is probably one of the most exciting places a naturalist will ever get to explore and certainly one of my favorites. It is a unique place, a fringe of both the sea and the land, a narrow ribbon between the great ocean and the land mass against which it laps, as well as a junction between both of these and the air. Add to all this the daily effects of the timetable of the tides and the seasons and you have quite a lot of "edges," each bringing its own survival challenges for the creatures that live there.

To help you get straight to the most useful sections of the book, depending on whether your toes are sinking into soft sand or being prickled by barnacles, the seashore habitat is broken down still farther—into rock pools, sandy shores, estuaries, and cliffs. But do not restrict yourself to these sections as there are no hard and fast definitions of each. For example, the beach you are on may be predominantly covered in rocks but there may be sandy stretches. Or there could be an estuary at one end of the beach, so there will be some overlap between each of the different habitats and the things you can do there.

I won't set out to tell you everything there is to know about this wonderful habitat. Not only would that be impossible, but just to get close would make the book so heavy you wouldn't stand a chance of getting it in your beach bag! So *Seashore* simply aims to kick start you in the right direction, opening a door onto a very special, exciting habitat and a lifetime of exploring. Go stick your head in a rock pool!

There is nothing like the nooks and crannies of a good rock pool.

The muddy ooze of an estuary is far from dreary—it is full of surprises.

Playing in the sand isn't all about sandcastles.

A puffin enjoying his view!

Life in stripes: zonation

Look at a rocky shore from the top of a cliff or walk from the strand line toward the sea and you cannot help but notice bands of different colors and textures that run up and down the beach. These bands represent where on the beach certain plants and animals live, and it is clear that life is not scattered randomly all over the shore. Certain species that cannot move about freely, such as barnacles and seaweeds, live in very specific places, and this is a reflection of what conditions they can tolerate between the tides.

These stripes are known as zones and all coasts have them, but they are much more obvious on rocky shores. There are four main zones—the splash zone, the lower shore, the middle shore, and the upper shore—and each one is determined by how much time they spend getting wet every day between the high and low tides. Page 8 tells you how the tides change every day and throughout the year, and also the cycles of the Sun, Earth, and Moon.

The best way to get to know the zones is by creating a simple beach map. This exercise is a very useful way to start to get to know the life between the tides, and you also start to see just how different life is in each zone.

To get a good picture of the beach, survey it at low tide. Stretch a ball of string from the top of the beach to the sea. Then for every yard of its length, write down what you see in a notebook. Are there barnacles? Are there limpets? What colors and different kinds of seaweeds can you see? Try to identify as much as possible from a good field guide.

The splash zone is the no-man's land of the shore. It is too dry for sea-living life, too wet and salty for those of the land. Here you may find a salt-tolerant plant, a woodlouse relative, and a few beetles, but the dominant life is that of the super tough lichens.

The upper shore is only covered with water at and around high tide, so the animals and plants here must be able to tolerate being exposed to the elements for most of the day, whether it is cold and rainy or hot and sunny. One of the most common indicators of this zone is channeled wrack seaweed. It can dry up and become crispy and black and then, once covered by the water, it will rehydrate like a bath sponge and become a succulent weed again.

The middle shore is where the numbers of species start to go up. The most obvious things that let you know you have arrived in the middle are the acorn barnacle and some of the most famous weeds, such as the rockweed and knotted wracks. This is the part of the beach that we are all familiar with and it is where most of us spend the largest amount of time.

The lower shore is a band that is only uncovered at low tide and only totally at the lowest of the low Spring tides. It is marked by a distinctive family of seaweeds called the Laminaria, which are the rubbery brown seaweeds that include the kelps.

Timetables of the tides

The tide—that's the rise and fall of the ocean—pretty much shapes life on the shore and affects how it behaves at certain times. Many shore creatures have life cycles tied in with these pulses of the ocean and the tide also affects how and when we can explore the shore. So just a little understanding of this will add another dimension to your activities and avoid disappointment. It will also help you to avoid getting trapped by an incoming tide.

Why does the sea come in and go out? Well, it's all down to the forces of gravity. The Moon and the Sun have a gravitational pull on the water in our oceans: imagine invisible strings attached to the sea tugging at the water and causing it to bulge out of shape. As the Moon rotates around the Earth every 28 days and the Earth spins around the Sun, the relative position of all three changes all the time, but in a predictable way. That is why we have tide timetables that you can get off the internet, a local newsagent, or the TV weather. It works just like a bus timetable, but it is more reliable.

When the Sun and Moon are in line with each other, the pull on the sea is greater than when they are at right angles. The greater the pull, the higher and lower the tides. When the Sun is closest to the Earth we get especially strong effects and these are known as Spring tides. This happens in March and September. These largest tides (and those that occur around them) are some of the most useful to the naturalist, because the water goes out so far on a Spring tide that it gives us a glimpse of life beyond the usual tidal limits. Exciting times for a shore explorer!

When the Sun and Moon are at right angles, the pull on the sea is at its weakest and we have what are known as Neap tides. At this time, the water sometimes hardly seems to move.

But the most important thing for a naturalist to know is the daily tidal pattern, which means you usually get two high tides and two low tides a day. These high tides are separated by approximately 12 hours and 25 minutes and that 25 minutes means that every day the high tides are later by about 50 minutes. This is the case with the open Atlantic on the US eastern seaboard, but the Gulf Coast and much of the West Coast experience mixed tides, with sequences ranging from high-high, low-low, to low-high, high-low.

Following the retreating water is a good way to work the beach. You can take your time and see the effects that the receding tide has on the animals that live there. It also means that you will have maximum time to explore the lowest parts of the shore before the tide turns and covers everything up again!

Take my advice

There are a few safety tips that I strongly suggest you think about when you are down on the coast.

Sun Protect yourself from the sun—wear a hat, sunscreen, and protective clothing.

Tides Be aware of how fast the tide is coming in! It is very easy to get distracted by what a limpet may be doing only to look up and find that huge expanse of rocky coast has become an island and, what's worse, you are on it! On some shallow, sloping shores, the tide can come in almost at walking pace, so it pays to do your research first. A beach that has a cliff can be dangerous, also—if you are not familiar with routes up and off the beach, the rising tide could cut you off, which is especially risky if the high water comes right up to the cliff base.

Getting wet Try to avoid swimming in fast-flowing water or at locations that are subject to strong tidal currents. It is all too easy to get swept away.

Buddy up—always swim with a partner. In case one of you gets into difficulties, it is twice as easy for two to get out of trouble as one.

Handy stuff for exploring

To explore the seashore doesn't require much equipment. Admittedly you will need to give a little thought to what you take with you, but the good news is that most of it can be improvized and made at home.

Big stick Acts as an extra leg, which is very useful for preventing you from falling into the sea and, as an added bonus, useful for lifting up curtains of weed.

Binoculars Not essential, but there is usually something to see out at sea. It may be some terns fishing, a passing seal, dolphin, or even a basking shark!

Burrow box (see page 44) A home-made tank that allows you to watch burrowing creatures in action. A little one works well for looking at smaller water creatures, especially in conjunction with a magnifying lens.

Clear plastic robust pots I find these useful when collecting frail and brittle specimens such as delicate shells, skate and ray egg cases, and sea urchins.

First aid kit Keep a fully equipped kit close by at all times, including insect repellent, sunscreen, antiseptic spray, and band aids.

Garden fork A small gardener's fork is easy to carry around, but if you are going for big worms and doing a lot of under-the-sand investigations, then a large fork will prove more useful.

Magnifying lens Useful to any naturalist, anywhere!

Mirror on a stick (see page 13) Handy little home-made device for looking underneath overhangs and ledges without cutting your knees on barnacles or by falling in. A whole new perspective on rock pools!

Nets A good robust net is vital. Forget those flimsy colored ones stuffed in the end of a bamboo cane found for sale in most beach shacks—they are good for nothing!

Non-slip, free-draining shoes/sandals Stops slippage, barnacle cuts on the toes and saves pain in case of treading on hidden glass or sea urchin spines. And if they drain, they are easily washed and won't stink the house out.

Notebook and pen/pencil Essential for noting down and keeping track of all your discoveries on the seashore.

Plastic tank Forget the traditional plastic bucket. It doesn't have clear sides and so you can't see in. Instead, take with you a small, clear plastic tank. Now you can see any animals you catch at their level.

Plastic ziploc bags Versatile and invaluable, you can put everything from pellets and smelly specimens to shells or your lunch in them.

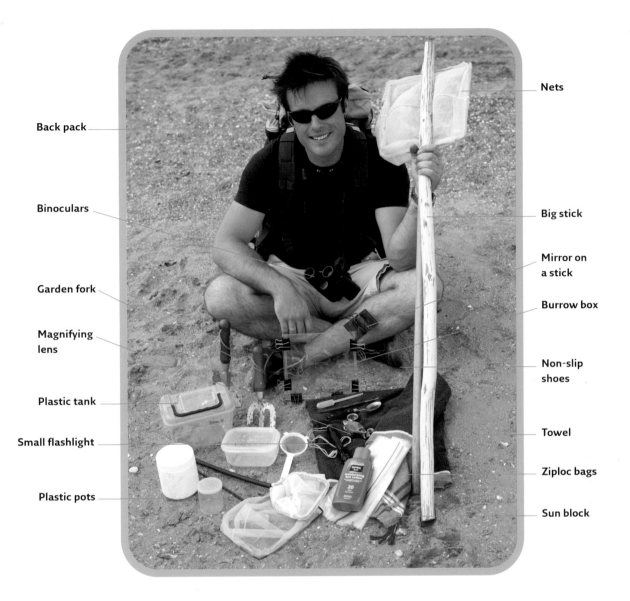

Back pack

Binoculars

Garden fork

Magnifying
lens

Plastic tank

Small flashlight

Plastic pots

Nets

Big stick

Mirror on
a stick

Burrow box

Non-slip
shoes

Towel

Ziploc bags

Sun block

Polarizing sunglasses Great for seeing into the water more clearly.

Small flashlight Useful for illuminating those dark cracks and crevices in rocks.
Sun block The combination of exposed environments and the way the Sun bounces back
off the water is dangerous. You will burn very quickly and easily, so slap it on!

Towel Things do get wet that shouldn't and that could be you or some equipment. Can
also be used as a shade to protect living specimens from the Sun.

Back pack To put it all in!

Rock pools

I still can't resist peering into these puddles of sea water or turning over a rock. The addiction is simple and this habitat is one of the most exciting and surprising places on planet Earth. To this day, almost every stone I turn reveals another creature that I have never seen before.

Each rock pool is unique. Those higher up the beach will be exposed for longer, and on a hot sunny day they will experience evaporation, meaning the water gets saltier. This, in turn, means less oxygen in the water for the creatures to breath. If it rains, the pools can become diluted to the point of almost being fresh water; this is very stressful for animals that are used to salty water. So, as a result, these rock pools are where the beach's real hard cases hang out; the rock pool specialists.

The farther down the shore you go, the less time is spent isolated from the sea and so the more stable the conditions. Here you will tend to find a greater variety of life, and in the very last pools to be exposed at the lowest Spring tides, you may even find truly ocean-going creatures that simply get caught out.

Over the course of the seasons, life in the pools changes and as well as year-round residents, some creatures make migrations to and from the rock pools to deeper water. Every tide that sweeps over the beach and then retreats again can bring with it fresh surprises, so you can never be totally sure of what you may find.

I always find that animals and plants that live underwater tend to look quite flat, boring, or just plain uncomfortable on dry land. Nowhere is this more obvious than at the seaside "rock pooling." So instead of turning over stone after stone you can make a naturalist's version of a dentist's mirror to allow you to look under overhanging rocks and in crevices. I call this quite simply a mirror on a stick.

Handy stuff: mirror on a stick

Use this extended mirror to bounce light into the shadows. I find it is one of the best ways to find egg cases of dog whelks and other creatures that want to keep out of harm's way.

2 Bend one end at right angles and attach to a travel shaver's mirror with reinforced duct tape (from a hardware store). Make a more solid handle by binding the other end with the duct tape.

1 Take 2 feet of thick but bendable wire, fold it in half and twist.

3 Use the mirror to shed light on those otherwise dark and sinister cracks and crevices.

4 Bend the wire into a right angle so you can look in all those rock pools. You can even get an idea of what the world is like looking up from a crab's point of view.

The baiting game

I remember going "crabbing" as a kid, hunting for crabs for my supper. This involved tossing bait into the pools and coming back later to scoop up the unfortunate crustaceans into a net. But I found that some of the bait was seemingly being pulled by an invisible force across the bottom of the pools while other pieces exploded into hundreds of fragments, which would then be shunted around rapidly, resembling underwater fireworks. Other bits had simply disappeared! Very soon I was gazing into the pools trying to figure out who the thieves were. It was at that moment I was hooked, and so I became a rock pool investigator.

Many of the residents of rock pools are opportunists—they take whatever they can, whenever they can. They are the scavengers and the waste disposal units of the sea. By placing bait in the pools you are actually recreating something that happens all the time in nature.

When a creature dies anywhere in any ecosystem on the planet, there are a whole host of other creatures ready to return the goodness its body contains back into the living system, and rock pools are no exception. Animals die here, and our coasts are also the last resting place for many other creatures that die at sea and are washed up. Believe me, a body in a rock pool will not last long. But don't just believe me, try it out for yourself.

Really, it's all about experimenting. Different baits may work better in different places and at different times, but the basic principle is the same. For best results, you need to spread the word to the rock pool community that bait has arrived, and you want the word to reach as many different creatures as quickly as possible.

Nick's trick

Use the smelliest bait possible and ideally one that contains an element of "soup"— soft stuff that will break up into tiny particles and get wafted around in the water currents.

1 Bring your own bait—the smellier the better, as this will waft around in the water and draw in creatures from farther away. I have used everything from scraps and trimmings that my local fishmonger has given me, like nice and smelly fish heads and tails, to bacon or ham that I have removed from my own sandwiches.

2 Attach your bait to a piece of string so that you can lift the bait out of the water if a particularly greedy or boisterous crab or fish comes along. Many scavengers, such as crabs and blennies, can be very greedy and will leave the scene altogether, taking your bait with them.

3 If the idea of handling smelly dead fish bits really fills you with disgust, there is a neat little trick that also works well using a jar of fish paste. Take the lid off your jar and stir up the contents a bit. Then cover with the mesh or old stocking and secure firmly with the rubber band.

4 Pop the jar into a rock pool and that's it! Just sit back and watch as the residents come scuttling.

Handy stuff: scavenger trap

Around areas where there is a fishing business, you may come across large rope and wooden structures used to catch crabs and lobsters. You can borrow this idea and make your own rock pool version.

The trap is made from a container, which lets the smell of your bait escape into the water. When the creatures come searching, they find their way in via a funnel. This then acts as a one-way valve, trapping them inside. The cheapest way to do this is with an old plastic soda bottle.

With the aid of your scavenger trap and a field guide you will soon be able to identify many different rock pool creatures.

Nick's trick

In an area where periwinkles or dog whelks are found, try dragging your bait around on a sandy bottom and watch what happens. These scavenging snails will follow the trail, siphons up, as they pick up the smell of the bait.

1 Take the bottle and cut off the top about 4in down (you might need to ask an adult to help you as this can be difficult). You will be left with a funnel and a trap box. Then make lots of small holes in the main part of the bottle.

2 Put some bait into the trap and insert the top of the bottle, neck end down. Fasten in place with strips of duct tape.

3 Search out some large, flat rocks and attach them to the bottle using string. They look like little packages and will weigh down your trap, which is important as a drifting trap spells death for all those caught inside. Plastic bottles are also one of the worst kinds of trash.

4 Position the trap in a rock pool and then leave for a few hours.

5 You will want to take a closer look at what you've caught, so carefully place your captives in an observation tank to study them.

Marvellous mollusks

These simple little cone-shaped shells are a familiar sight on a wave-beaten rocky shore. Their shell design and body shape are perfect for resisting the constant battering of the ocean. These mollusks have a large circular foot, which allows them to clamp tight to the rocks on which they live, making them very hard to pry off the rocks without doing any damage.

A combination of their habitual behavior and the abrasive action of their shells on the rock means that they will often wear away the rock's surface, leaving small circular pits as evidence of their home base. You can also sometimes see grazing trails similar to those left by their land-based relatives, the garden snails.

You might think that watching limpets is about as much fun as watching paint dry! But you can turn even the dullest beach into a study zone. What do you know about these little mollusks? Not a lot, OK. So follow the steps opposite and you will learn a little bit more. This technique is used by biologists to study the movement of all kinds of animals.

Nick's tricks

* You can take limpets by surprise! If you catch one with its shell slightly raised and are quick, you can flick them off with one deft movement of your hand, giving you a chance to see the animal itself. Remember to put them back exactly where you found them.

* To see a limpet even more clearly, pop one inside a clear-sided observation tank and you will get a rock's point of view of these tough little rock pool characters that are often taken for granted.

> quick-drying, non-water-based model paint in any bright color
> paintbrush
> paper
> pencil

1 Using the model paint and paintbrush, mark a few limpets on a rock with a tiny blob of colored paint.

2 Draw a map of the rocks and the positions of your color-coded limpets.

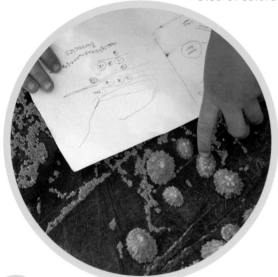

3 Return the next day. Have they moved? Most of them probably won't have, but some may well have moved a surprising distance. To find out just how much they do shuffle about, return to the same spot at night on a low tide. Try to find your mollusks then— you'll be surprised ...

Take it further

* Don't feel you should limit your marking studies to limpets. You can try similar studies with any hard-shelled creatures, such as periwinkles and crabs.

* Use different-colored paints for limpets on different rocks. With time, will they intermingle?

Shell collecting

The seashore is a tough place to live for a soft-bodied creature. There is the continuous pounding of the waves and the constant threat from predators from the sea, land, and air. Then, for those creatures that live on the main part of the beach, there is the threat of being left out in the open, exposed to the drying effects of the wind and the sun. Five minutes of summer sun could turn a succulent, soft sea slug into a crisp!

One easy fix for all of these survival problems is to live in your own portable, environmental protection suit, which is exactly what a sea shell is to a snail!

Any strand line, anywhere in the world, will probably have some of these beautiful structures, cast up from the ocean, their original molluskan creators long gone. Be warned, though, shell collecting is very addictive. Once you have started walking a strand line, you will be surprised just how far you have strolled, eyes down searching for the next piece of natural treasure!

Nick's trick

Shells are made from a material called calcium carbonate or chalk, which the mollusks (that's the scientific term for all snails) collect from sea water and their food. This chalk is then built into the shell. If you look at different kinds of shells, you can see that they have lines or layers, which are like the rings inside a tree and show how the snail has grown.

Fab fact

To stop shells losing that sparkly beauty that made you stoop down to pick them up in the first place, try washing them with a soft brush and soapy water when you get home. Once they have dried, rub them with a fine mineral oil or give them a coat of thin, water-based varnish. I prefer the oil, as varnish is permanent and gives a false impression of the shell's real texture.

If you wish to collect shells, bear in mind the following points:

> **Do not buy shells from trinket shops.** Many of these have been collected in the wild, the rightful owner having been pulled out and killed, just to sell to a tourist as a pretty ornament to place upon their bathroom shelf. Also, the shells of some mollusks have been over-collected and they are now among the most endangered creatures on earth.

> **When collecting shells, make sure there is definitely no one at home.** Some mollusks can retreat a long way into their shells and may not be visible at first, and some may also be second-hand homes, inhabited by hermit crabs.

> **If you are in any doubt, pop your find in some sea water** and watch it for a moment. If there is a resident creature, it will usually relax a little and peek out.

Take it further

* As with all collections, it is always a good idea to label any shells you find as this stops them becoming just ornaments that gather dust. Writing down the date, location, and identity of the species of mollusk that once made it helps you to remember their names. The labels also bring back memories of the beach and the experience that day brought to you. Who knows, maybe one day your collection will be of use to science!

* Stick your labels onto the shells with tape or glue or place a loose label in a clear bag along with your shell.

See inside a sea shell

One way to take your sea shell interest further is to think about shells from the viewpoint of the creatures that once owned them. That small, sculptured piece of calcium carbonate is not just a beautiful form, it also has a function. Where the mollusk lives and what it does are all reflected in the shape of the shell. It is, after all, both a home and a skeleton.

The smooth, bullet-like shape of a tellin shell is designed to slip through the sand and the mud, whereas the spikes and spines of a prickly cockle are used to hold the animal in place in shifting sands. In other species, like some limpets, ridges give weeds and other plants a footing, helping to camouflage the creature underneath.

You can plainly see the two halves that make up the shell of a bivalve such as this. The hinge is delicate and they often get separated once the animal inside dies.

These are a selection of proper snails or gastropods, a bit like the ones you might find in your backyard at home.

This is a chalky bone of a cuttlefish, a specialized shell that acts like an internal skeleton for these, the most advanced of mollusks.

Fab facts

Basically shells come in three designs. **Bivalves**, which means two halves. These include familiar species such as clams and mussels. These animals are either attached to a surface by strong threads of material called byssus, which are produced by the animal, or are buried in the mud or sand. **Gastropods**, which means belly-foot. These are much more like the familiar garden gastropods and are the true sea snails. Their shells are one-piece affairs, some with complicated whirls and others with simple domes. An example would be the whelk. **Chitons**, or coat-of-mail shells, can sometimes be found stuck to rocks. Because their shell breaks up when they die, you rarely find a complete one washed up on the beach.

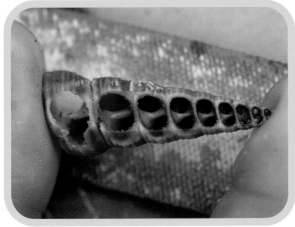

1 Take your shell and, with a firm grip, rub it backward and forward on the abrasive paper or file. You will eventually start to wear through the shell.

2 Keep it up and not only will you reveal the inside chambers and their shapes, but you will see how thick the shell is and be able to look at the growth lines.

3 The effort required does depend on the size and thickness of the shell. Do not be too ambitious to start with, choose a smallish specimen. If you want to deal with the larger, thicker shells, you may need to gently clamp your shell in a vice and use a large flat file instead. Better still, if you know anyone with a mechanical grinding wheel, ask them to do it for you.

Take it further

File shells from different kinds of beaches. Is there anything you notice about the thickness of a shell from an exposed shore compared to one of the same species living on a sheltered beach?

Handy stuff: underwater window

Even in the relatively shallow and clear water of rock pools it can still be quite a job seeing into the water clearly. This is because the surface of the water bounces light around in many different directions and the more ripples caused by water movement and wind, the worse it is. So try out a pair of polarizing sun glasses, or you can make your own window into the rock pool world for a few nickels— and it's really easy to make.

By pressing the window against the surface of the water, it cuts out ripples and the raised edge cuts out the glare. You can make your underwater window out of any materials, like old cans (although you must cover any edges with duct tape) and plastic tubs, with the bottom cut out of them and a thin piece of transparent film, such as cellophane or plastic wrap, stretched over the hole and secured. But the best thing to use is an ice-cream container (see opposite).

If you can't construct yourself an underwater viewer, you can, of course, use a diving mask in a similar way or, better still, you could wear it in the way it was designed for, and get wet (see page 26).

The underwater window is a good way to see through the ripples to the watery world below.

YOU WILL NEED

> **an old ice-cream container**
> **scissors**
> **dark gray duct tape (or black plastic waterproof paint and a paintbrush)**
> **plastic wrap**

2 Repeat with the main part of the tub—this will become the frame for the viewer.

3 To eliminate side glare and light, and improve viewing when looking through what was the bottom of the original ice-cream tub, cover the sides with duct tape (or paint them with the plastic waterproof paint if you are using this instead).

1 Take your tub and carefully cut out the center of the lid—this will hold the plastic wrap in place.

Nick's trick

Why not try using this device in conjunction with bait? Rest a small piece of smelly fish or meat in the underwater viewer and see what it attracts.

4 Stretch the plastic film tightly over the top of the tub and keep in place with the lid.

5 You now have an underwater viewing device that, when pressed to the surface, allows you to see clearly the aquatic goings on of the world beneath the surface. The beauty of this design is that if the window gets damaged, you can replace it very easily. All you need to do now, is find yourself a rock pool.

Snorkeling for softies

When I was a young naturalist, the idea of getting in the water terrified me. I'm not sure if I was afraid of sharks or whether the water just seemed so cold and unfriendly. But it took me a long time to get in the water properly. Looking back on it, there was nothing to be afraid of—just the unknown. However, from this fear I developed a compromise between my fascination and my fear. I now call it "snorkeling for softies," although in all honesty, I still do it, as it does have some unique underwater attractions that cannot be had in any other way.

This approach to snorkeling has a number of different levels, depending on your experience. It is a good way to slowly get someone who is nervous about swimming in the sea to get comfortable with the things that live beneath its surface. All you really need is a mask and a snorkel.

> **Beginner's level: see opposite.**

> **Intermediate level:** this requires rock pools that are large enough to actually climb into. On a sunny day the Sun's energy warms up the pools, so it is rather like swimming in the bath, even if it is one stuffed full of colored seaweeds and animals. You can paddle around for hours with your mask and snorkel, looking under rock overhangs and having plenty of adventures. Friends and family might make fun of you, but you could become the next great sea explorer.

> **Advanced level:** you might eventually be inspired to take up SCUBA diving. There are courses at local swimming pools or at certain beaches. You might have to be a certain age, though, and you will certainly need to be a strong swimmer.

Scared of what lurks under the surface? Don't be—grab a mask and snorkel and get your head wet!

1

For the beginner's level, seek out an inviting-looking stretch of rock next to a rock pool. You might want to lie on your towel to make the whole occasion as comfortable as possible. Slip on the mask and snorkel.

2

Slowly lower your head into the water. Once you have got used to the temperature—and you will, trust me—this is a great way of seeing rock pool creatures like shrimps and anemones without disturbing them. You can even carry out some of the other activities in this book without removing any animal from its home.

YOU WILL NEED

> **your beach towel**
> **a bathing suit**
> **snorkel and mask**

Nick's trick

Knee pads, such as those used by gardeners, builders, or skateboarders, are handy if you are going to spend a lot of time on all fours. Barnacles will soon reduce your knees to shreds otherwise.

Blobs!

Look carefully in a rock pool, under the ledges and edges, under seaweed, even buried in the sand, and you will find a range of peculiar creatures. At best, they resemble a kind of wobbly, stumpy, stalked flower or, at worse, a semi-digested gummy bear that has been stuck to a rock's surface. These are the sea anemones and there are many different kinds.

Some species cannot cope with being out of the water for long and are always found in permanent or deep water, while others have adapted to life in the rock pools. Despite looking a bit like small plants, anemones are, in fact, animals and even though they may look uninteresting (and admittedly they do not have the charisma of a crab), they are fascinating little predators. I just wish it was easier to see what they get up to, but most of the coolest things about an anemone either happen very slowly or they occur at a microscopic level!

Fab facts

* The real enemy of these little softies is the constant threat of dehydration if they get exposed by the retreating water. Some anemones deal with this problem by "swallowing" a big gulp of sea water and storing it within their body. On exposure they then bring in all their tentacles, reducing their surface area, and slowly dribble out the sea water, keeping themselves moist and supple until the tide returns to cover them up and life resumes as normal.

* Another cool fact is that waste is passed back out of the mouth—these animals do not have a proper bottom!

The frilled anemone is one of the common rock pool species. But it can't turn into a blob and survive out of water for long.

1 First you need to find an anemone that is submerged and has all of its feeding tentacles splayed out. This means it is relaxed and looking for food.

2 Take a tiny fragment of meat, maybe from your sandwich, and drop it into the anemone. Watch what happens—very quickly the tentacles grab the food and pass dinner into the anenome's mouth, which is a hole in the middle of the frill.

3 Find another anemone and just touch its tentacles with your finger. It feels soft and sticky, right? Well, that stickiness is to do with lots of tiny stinging cells that are too delicate in most species for us to actually feel.

Take it further

* On the anemone's skin there are lots of little sacs that are way too small to be seen with the naked eye. Each one contains a small barb attached to a thread; the whole set-up is just like a harpoon gun. The harpoon is fired when the anemone tastes food, an enemy, or even another anemone! The barb gets stuck in the flesh of the creature, and the anemone then drags it in. When you pass your finger through the anemone this is what is happening, you are being shot by loads of tiny harpoons!

* These little harpoons (or nematocysts as they are called) are even used against neighboring anemones if they get too close. Although they look like plants, they can actually move, even if it is very, very slowly. They creep about on the rock's surface to reach better feeding areas, find mates, or to get into a place that is less exposed.

* If one bumps into another, they "arm wrestle" with their tentacles. In some species, such as the beadlet anemone, the blue beadlets (which are full of stinging cells), swell up and sting the opponent. In these slow-mo battles, large ones usually beat small ones and reds beat the greens!

* Despite seeming to be blob bullying blob, this behavior means they spread out and there is plenty of food for everyone.

Crab hunting

One habitat that insects haven't taken control of is the sea. Why? Well, it's because the crustaceans were there first. The most famous crustaceans that you will come across on your rambles among the rocks pools are the crabs, prawns, and barnacles.

The universal pastime among younger people who visit a rocky shore (and something I did too), is to run for the nearest rock pool and start turning each little universe upside down on a neverending quest to catch as many crabs as possible and stuff them in a bucket! Not much fun for the crabs and really a bit of a pointless and destructive activity. But there is so much more that can be learned from these armor-plated scavengers of the shore, than how many will fit in your bucket.

In the rock pool environment, the top three crabs that most "crabbers" will be familiar with are:
> The green crab.
> The beautiful swimming blue crab.
> The Atlantic rock crab.
All can be found by turning over rocks or baiting pools.

The green crab is the most widespread because it is so tolerant of changes in temperature, salinity, and oxygen, and can be found higher up the beach than any other crab. The others are more restricted, so the best place to look for them is in larger, more permanent rock pools lower down the shore.

Nick's trick

My top tip for any rock pooling ramble is to take a small plastic tank with clear sides with you. Pop any crab you can find into the water and you will be able to see eye to eye and get a feel for what being a crab is all about. They will liven up and you will be able to see them so much better than when in their own element.

1 The Pacific hermit crab is one interesting specimen. Peer into a pool and you will notice that some of the rough-shelled winkles in residence seem a little livelier than others. Pick up one of these high-speed winkles and do not be surprised if you see some reddish orange legs and beady eyes on stalks. These are hermit crabs and they recycle old sea shells. As they grow, they constantly need to find larger accommodation.

2 You are unlikely to see them swap into new shells, but to improve your chances, put a variety of different-sized shells and a hermit crab in your plastic tank. Now for the difficult bit—you need to persuade your crab to leave its house. Try gently pulling on its front limbs. This can be a little bit like a tug of war, as the crab often grips the inside of the shell. Blowing on it is also a trick that works well.

3 Once you have extracted your crab, take a good look. The back end of its body is a soft and vulnerable sack. You can also see the limbs that have been turned into grippers. Place your upset crustacean back into the tank and watch what happens. The crab scuttles around, measuring the shells for size with its legs. When it selects its new home, it rapidly reverses into it, panic over.

Flip over a crab and you may find one that is carrying an egg mass around with it.

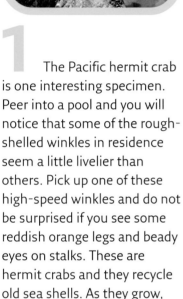

Take it further

* See if you can find more of the over 200 different kinds of true crab that live around US shores—and that number doesn't even include the lobsters and their relatives!

* Diseased crabs cannot moult and often stand out as their carapaces are encrusted with tube worms.

* Look out for green crabs in "berry." These are the female crabs that are carrying their batches of salmon-pink or brown eggs around with them under their tail flaps.

Crab catching

To catch a crab, take a household or soil sieve to the areas of mud, sand, or gravel exposed at lowest tide and you stand a good chance of turning up a few common species, as well as lots of interesting worms and burrowing bivalves. Sometimes the cutest crab can be found here—the thumb nail crab is small (about 1in) and, yes, looks surprisingly like a thumb nail!

Without getting your fingers nipped by the pincers (see opposite), lift up your crab or turn it over. You will notice a triangular plate pointing up towards the center of the crab's "face," between its eyes. This is actually a flap, a little like the tail of a lobster that has been folded back on itself to protect the crab's underside, delicate gills and all. In a female crab, this flap is used to attach her eggs to her underside and is shaped like a triangle with a much broader base. Males, on the other hand, have a much narrower flap. It may take a little practice and you may need to look at two crabs together to compare, but eventually you will train your eye to see the difference.

We rightly fear our fingers falling into the defensive grasp of crabs. The calipers that in a healthy crab are positioned at the ends of the first pair of legs are very useful tools, not only as feeding aids—a kind of a knife, fork, and spoon in one—but they are also very handy weapons against other crabs and predators. And as far as a crab is concerned, you are nothing but a big predator that is about to try for his life. Never mind how well meaning or interested in him you are, he will do what crabs are famous for and nip at the slightest provocation.

The best way to avoid a nip is not to touch. But at some point you are going to want or need to pick one up. The hardest thing is getting to grips with your crab in the first place as they will do everything to out-maneuver you and run to safety. The best ways to handle one are shown opposite.

The common shore crab is also known as the green crab because it is mainly green as an adult.

If you have a particularly large specimen, the best thing you can do is to cover your animal quickly with an old rag or flannel (quite a useful thing to carry with you anyway). Throw it over the crab so that it cannot see you. This will mean it will relax and put its pincers down for a few seconds. You will then be able to regain control while minimizing the chance of getting nipped.

1 Place your hand flat over the front end of the crab and push down firmly. Then use your free hand to gently but firmly grip the base of its carapace at the back, just above the last leg joint. It may struggle and seem very close to pinching you, but trust your crab hold and you will remain unhurt—and your crab can be viewed easily!

2 Another way to pick up your crab is to hold its carapace on either side between thumb and forefinger. What to do if you mess up and find yourself experiencing the crustacean crush? Well, do not panic, no amount of pulling or tugging will help persuade your crab to see sense. Instead, put your hand, crab and all, in water and it will release its grip before scuttling off to safety.

Take it further

* Why not collect crab carapaces? As a crab grows, it sheds its external skeleton in the same way as insects and spiders. These dried remains can often be found washed up on the strand line.

* To tell the difference between a molted exoskeleton and a dead crab, sniff the remains! Dead crabs quickly become smelly, whereas a shed skin will be less upsetting to your nasal passages and will also have pale, hollow-looking eye stalks. Look at the old skin and you will be able to see:

> How the "tail" or abdomen of the crab is like a lobster's or shrimp's that has been curled up beneath its body.
> The positions of the fluffy gill filaments inside the skin.
> The variation in colors and patterns between species.

Handy stuff: plankton net

Sea water is not just water, it is a living soup and that is why there are so many creatures large and small that go to great lengths to suck this soup through their bodies to filter it. Everything from a barnacle, a peacock worm, and cockle—even a blue whale—is sieving the water constantly to extract food for fuel to live from it. The coolest thing about this fuel is that it really is a rich mixture of tiny microscopic plants, which in turn are eaten by microscopic animals; some of these animals are the ugly-looking babies of more familiar creatures, such as crabs, barnacles, and even fish.

Some are so small you can usually only see them through a microscope, but fortunately other plankton is quite large and it is possible to see some of these delicate creatures, if not with the naked eye, then at least using a good hand lens. You can either use your eyes and simply scoop up anything you feel is interesting, or you can increase your chances and target the microscopic hoards by making your own plankton net, which is easy!

YOU WILL NEED

> **pair of tights or a stocking**
> **scissors**
> **strong thread**
> **needle**
> **wire hoop**
> **pole or broom handle**
> **duct tape**
> **plastic bottle**
> **string**

This is plankton magnified for you to be able to enjoy. You get a mouthful of this when you swallow sea water!

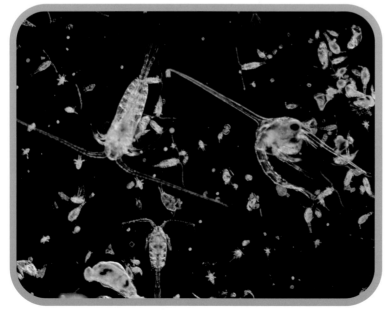

1 First of all you need to be nice to your sister, mom, or aunt and get her to give you one of her old pairs of tights or a stocking (one without too many holes in it). You just need one leg.

2 If you are using tights, cut off one of the legs and sew the open end onto the wire hoop (if you are using a stocking, there will be an open end all ready and waiting). The stitches don't have to be beautiful but they do have to be strong.

3 Attach the wire to your stout pole or broom handle using plenty of duct tape. Then cut off the foot end of the stocking.

4 Slide the foot end over the plastic container and tie a piece of string around the neck of the bottle. Fasten the stocking to the bottle with plenty more duct tape. Your plankton net is complete!

5 To use your plankton net, find some open water. The net won't work unless water is flowing through it. Generate the movement yourself by towing the net through the water. I have even had pretty good results by dangling and towing my net from the end of a pier.

6 Once you have raised your net, empty the contents of the jar into an observation pot and then use the plankton viewer on page 37 to look at the mini micro-monsters that you have caught.

The fine, fiddly, and frail

Whether it is the delicate body of a comb jelly, a shrimp found lurking in the weed, or the gentle feeding limbs of a barnacle, it is very easy to miss the hidden micro beauty of this semi-transparent world. Here is one very cool little trick that allows you to see all that is going on.

These are the hard homes of spiral tube worms, which you can find among seaweed—espcially kelp (see page 46). If you put them in water and look carefully, you'll see the little guys moving out of their shells.

Nick's tricks

* Look for a stone with a colony of live barnacles on it—the dead ones have usually lost their front door valves and so have a gaping hole.

* Place the stone in a tank of water and watch carefully.

* You will see the doors open and out will pop a pair of feathery organs, which will appear to grab something. These are the limbs of the barnacle and they have a feathery structure to increase their surface area to trap and sieve particles out of the water.

* Many aquatic animals use this form of feeding, but the barnacle is especially good at getting its dinner.

* Note the temperature of the water and count the feeding motions. What happens if you change the temperature of the water?

* Watch the feeding by squirting little bits of liquidized food into the water using an eyedropper. What does the barnacle prefer?

1 Take your jar or tank and partially cover the back and sides with black construction paper. You might also want to make a lid from the paper to cut out light from above. Then fill with sea water —here we used the water from our plankton catcher. If you have caught a particular specimen, place it in the jar or tank.

2 Using your flashlight, light up your catch from below and slightly from behind at an angle. By looking at it through the portion of the sides not covered, the back lighting will make all the finest details, like hairs, bristles, and feeding limbs, stand out.

3 You can also take this opportunity to peer closely at your exciting catches through a magnifying glass. It is amazing what you will notice when everything is so very much larger.

Sandy shores

For the naturalist there are two main kinds of soft shore: those with boulders and pebbles, and those with sand or mud. It is easier for the sea to move some of these than others.

On shores where the loose particles are big, like boulders, all the smaller stuff is carried away by the waves. This leaves the shore quite exposed, which is important knowledge for the naturalist, because the more exposed the shore is, the less wildlife can be found. So there is much less wildlife on pebble beaches than on sheltered beaches made of rich sands and muds.

Not only are sandy beaches full of wildlife, but the constantly shifting sands throw up lots of problems that sandy shore creatures have overcome with some pretty neat adaptations, making them some of the most bizarre creatures to look at.

The problem is trying to find them! They are below the surface of the sand, where the temperature is relatively constant and they remain nice and damp while waiting for the tide to return. But remember, there are many different kinds of sand: coarse sand, soft fine sand, and muddy sand. And you also get zones on sandy shores, just as you do on rocky shores, only they are less obvious. So you will find different creatures in different places, depending on how much drying out they can tolerate and the sort of sand they prefer.

In windy locations you will find another interesting habitat on soft, sandy shores: sand dunes. These are becoming more rare as parking lots and paths are built for tourists, and those that exist are often eroded by people climbing, walking, and riding through them. But in a perfect dune system, you will find a secret world of sheltered suntraps.

Look for clues to the creatures to be found buried beneath the surface by scouring the strand line for shells and remains.

The bleached white test of a heart urchin.

The lugworm's back door ...

This ragworm has gone for a forage on the surface of the wet sand, leaving behind a tell-tale trail.

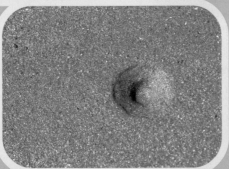

... and his front door!

Beachcombing

This is what you call walking along for mile after mile with your head bent down scouring the strand (or "wrack") line for things of interest—and for the naturalist, those things are usually in plentiful supply. The strand line may at first sight look like an unruly tangle of junk and seaweed. But there is always something of interest on this line of debris thrown onto the shore by the ocean. It is a world full of surprises and, because you just never know what you'll find next, beachcombing is one of those hobbies that becomes strangely addictive.

Look at the strand line as if you were a detective looking for clues as to what is out at sea. These days, it may seem that manmade trash or flotsam and jetsam dominate, but look beyond the eyesore and the strand line is rich picking for a naturalist. It can be more fruitful at certain times than at others. For example, if there has been a high tide at night, first thing in the morning is good, since any soft animals or creatures that have been washed up will not have been scavenged yet by gulls and dogs.

But the best time of all is the first high tide after a really strong gale at sea. When this happens, many creatures—often those rarely seen at any other time—get torn from their home in the water and find themselves stranded.

To be a star beachcomber, all you need is a good pair of eyes and big pockets. It may, however, also be worth taking some plastic bags and boxes to put any specimens in along with you.

Whelk egg cases are also known as sea wash balls, as sailors used to wash with them, rather like using a sponge. They are laid by whelks in deeper water on the sea bed. Look for the developing little whelks inside each of the off-white egg cases. Each contains over ten eggs but only one will survive to adulthood, as the first to hatch eats its developing siblings. Sometimes you can find crabs and squat lobsters hiding in the folds.

If you find a piece of driftwood riddled with lots of holes, these could be the burrows of woodborers (a kind of crustacean) or shipworms. Shipworms have long, worm-like bodies and their shells have a kind of drill bit to help them bore into dead wood. Use a pen knife to cut into the wood to see the animals themselves.

Mermaid's purses are the egg cases of skates and rays. Usually they would be attached to a rock or weed, but occasionally they are torn free and end up on the beach. Some will have hatched naturally, but others may still have the developing baby inside, either living or dead. Hold a flashlight behind them to see if you can make out the shape of the animal inside.

Watch out!

Because anything that gets dumped at sea, deliberately or otherwise, can be found on a beach somewhere, be careful and do not mess with strange objects or containers that may have something in them. Also watch out for oil, tar, and broken glass.

Catching sand-living creatures

Soft shores are constantly shifting and that means that if you live there, your environment will keep moving around you between the tides. This can be good news, especially if you eat algae that is wafted around as a result, because you do not have to go hunting for something to eat. But you do have to avoid being wafted about or eaten yourself.

So many sand-living creatures do everything they can to stay in control of their position. For something like a clam or any other bivalve mollusk, being exposed at high or low tide will mean becoming a snack for any passing oystercatcher or fish. For most of these mollusks, then, life is all about staying well and truly buried and hidden, but at the same time getting the opportunity to feed.

I think of these creatures as little vacuum cleaners. They have a tube called the inhalant siphon, which sucks in water and food, and they have another that blows the waste water out, called an exhalant siphon. The mollusk in the middle is the motor that pumps the water in and out, and it also acts as a filter, taking out of the muck any items of food that the mollusk can eat.

Different species use their body designs in different ways. Some have long, flexible siphons that can actively move through the sand and also probe around on the surface above, sucking up the sediment that lies on the surface. Others have much shorter siphons and rely on filtering the sea water itself. Even though it looks like it doesn't have many nutrients, sea water is, in reality, like a very thin, watered-down soup.

A common cockle with its beautiful ridged shell.

Fab fact

In rich and productive places, you can get huge numbers of cockles: over 1000 per square yard! That's one crowded neighborhood and it works in perfect unison with the pulse of the tides. When it's in, they are all sucking and filtering away, and when the tide is out, they take time out to digest their collections. That really is life tied to the tides!

1 Dig and sieve around on a soft shore and you will find various bivalve mollusks. They may give themselves up by leaving tell-tale marks on the surface (see page 39), but there are also many other smaller species that do not.

2 Now there is some fun that can be had with these little guys, which also gives you some clues as to how they make a living. Turn out your mollusks into an observation tank filled with sea water and place some sand in the bottom. Study them carefully.

3 After a while, you will notice sand trails leading from the tellin shells' bottoms ...

Take it further

Some tellin and furrow shells have incredibly long, spaghetti-like siphons while others, like clams, have short but wide siphons, which are used to filter the water. Here is a good way to see their feeding technique.

* Place a few clams into a dish of sea water and sand. Then make up a mixture of brewer's yeast with some water in a separate container, making sure it is nice and cloudy. Suck some up in an eyedropper and squirt over the clams' extended feeding siphons.

* The yeast is like food and the mollusk should suck this in through one end and send the clean filtered water out of the other. This shows you exactly how they filter sea water and it also tells you which siphon is which!

* Try this out on a variety of species and note down what you find out. The brewer's yeast can be used to feed any filter-feeding creature you choose to view, from the humble mussel to fan worms.

Handy stuff: burrow box

This simple kit has two very distinct uses, depending on its size. Make a large one for watching burrowing worms or mollusks (see opposite), while a smaller one can be kept in your pocket for instant use for observing small creatures that you have just hooked out of the water.

To help see the trails that a clamworm or clam will leave in your burrow box, add plaque detector (the same stuff dentists give you to turn your plaque pink or blue and which is available at most drug stores) to the sand. Any bacteria that are resting on the sand's surface will be stained too. It's just a simple way of showing you life forms that would otherwise remain invisible to the human eye. Watch how your clam sucks up those bacteria!

The secret of success lies in making sure you set up the burrow box so that its occupant is happy. As well as the clamworm and clam described here, you can use it to view the mud-loving shrimp that goes by the name of *Nereis virens*, which is commonly found in estuaries (see also page 59).

Take it further

Make your burrow box permanent by sealing the tubing in place with clear silicon sealant (available from hardware stores), and then you can get rid of the binder clips.

1 Take the two sheets of clear, hard plastic and insert the rubber tubing between them. The rubber needs to run around three of the four edges.

2 Use the binder clips to keep the rubber tubing in place. They need to be positioned at even distances around the edge of the plastic.

3 A perfect animal for your burrow box is a clamworm, one of the big game animals and the sort of creature every whimbrel would dream of catching. Gently dig between the wiggly cast and the indentation that it is always paired with (see page 39). You will have to dig deep and be gentle to avoid damaging your specimen.

4 Once you have your worm, fill the burrow box with sediment and sand from the area where you caught your worm. Then place the worm on the surface, and watch it burrow. How long does it take for its excavations?

5 After just ten minutes, this clamworm turned around and buried itself completely. You can still see him safe under the sand's surface.

Studying seaweeds

You may think of seaweed as being that green or brown stuff that you throw at your friends or slip and nearly break your neck on! Well, yes it is that, but it is also so much more. Nearly every plant you see on the shore is seaweed, and all of them belong to a group of plants called algae.

There are many different kinds of seaweed and they come in a variety of colors, such as brown, green, and red. Also, different species can handle different amounts of time out of the water and so are the main contributors to the character of the different tidal zones. Like any habitat on earth, the types of weed often reflect the types of creatures living in each zone.

Wracks are some of the best known of the seaweeds and probably one of the most numerous on rocky shores, as rocks are the perfect place for them to stick their holdfasts. Of all the wracks, knotted wrack and wrack weed are the best known. But there are many other kinds of wrack that live in the middle zone that have "bladders," as well as a few other types of weed. For starters, there are serrated, channel, knotted, and twisted wracks. If you walk over a carpet of the stuff, they often sound like bubble wrap popping. But have you ever thought about what the bladders actually do?

Look at a beach exposed by the tide and the weed forms a tangle, lying in flat expanses, draped over the rocks. But when the tide comes in, each little bladder pulls the frond to which it is attached up toward the surface. Air in these bladders work in the same way as a life jacket or a ship's buoy. They are floats. All the wracks "stand up" to get the fronds as close to the light as possible, where they do what all plants do best, and that's harness the Sun's energy and turn it into food.

Not just a messy mass of slimy seaweed, this is also home to many creatures.

1 Squeeze one piece of knotted wrack between your fingers and make it pop; then resist the urge to find another one and repeat!

From green sea lettuce (left) to the leathery, winged kelp (above), seaweeds come in a huge variety of shapes and colors.

Take it further

* Take a stick or the handle of your net and flip up some of the shrouds of wrack as they lie on the rocks or flop on the sand. You will often see all kinds of creatures hurrying for cover, from crabs to worms, even fish.

* Investigate their surface and you will discover many other creatures feeding and sheltering on the fronds. When the tide is out, these mats of weed provide a great place to hide from predatory eyes.

* The slippery, slimy film that coats the weeds is there to keep the moisture inside the plant but it also keeps its surroundings moist. As a result, many animals hide in it to escape the drying effects that the air and the elements can have on the exposed shore.

2 Take a piece of wrack and place it in a white tray full of water and sit and watch. See how many creatures crawl out of it. You may find eggs of rock pool creatures, too. Look closer and you will notice encrusted animals such as sea mats, tunicates, and spiral tube worms (see page 36), which live in small, white, curly tubes. Using a magnifying lens you may get to see the animals feeding and filtering the water.

Preserving your seaweeds

The smallest and least fleshy of the seaweeds can make quite beautiful displays, which is a great way to get to know them and, of course, to take back a souvenir of your visit to the shore. It certainly beats a stick of rock or a postcard!

Nick's trick

On some beaches, particularly after a storm, you will find the Big Daddies of the seaweed world, the kelps. If you find some, see if you can find its floats and the spidery looking holdfast, which grips the rocks. Look further and prod around with a pocket knife and you may find living creatures that have become stranded along with this giant algae. Pay particular attention to the "roots" or holdfast.

* You can also make a musical instrument, or kelp horn, by cutting the stem and then making a round hole in the float or the top of the hollow stem. Take it home and bend the kelp into the final shape you wish your instrument to be. Then put it somewhere warm and dry to set. Once it is dry, hollow out any of the fibrous pith using a piece of wire, pipe cleaners, and bottle brush to clean it out.

* Now you have your kelp horn, you just have to work out how to play it! Try placing your lips against the mouth piece and blowing as you would a trumpet, making a sound as if you were blowing a raspberry! Okay, it's not so musical, but it's a fun way of making a noise and in some parts of the world it's used as a signalling device.

YOU WILL NEED

- **a tray**
- **water**
- **watercolor paper**
- **pencil**
- **paintbrush**
- **blotting paper**
- **newspaper**
- **some heavy books or stones when you get home**

1 Fill your tray with water and then float the seaweed fronds, arranging them to look as good as possible.

2 Carefully slide the watercolor paper underneath your specimen, taking care to disturb it as little as possible. If you need to, do a bit of rearranging with the end of the paintbrush.

3 The next part takes some practice if your specimens are not to slip and slide back into the tray with the water (two people might make the job easier). Slowly lift the paper out of the tray so the water drains away leaving the weed in place on the wet paper. Once again, use the paintbrush to gently push, pull, and prod your weed into its final resting position. Then tip the paper slightly to remove any excess water.

4 Cover the seaweed with blotting paper and store it flat until you get home. Once indoors, change the blotting paper and if you have collected other seaweeds, stack them all up, placing sheets of newspaper between each and heavy books or stones on top. Change the newspaper daily and after two weeks, your specimens will be fully dried and fixed in position.

5 You can now either store them in a scrap book or, if you are feeling particularly proud of yourself, frame them and hang them up, being aware that bright light makes your specimens fade very quickly. Try to identify your seaweeds and write their name, date of collection, and the location on the sheet of watercolor paper.

Sand hoppers

The concept of a pitfall trap to catch creatures that roam around on the surface of the ground is not a very strange one to the naturalist. We use them to catch many different kinds of creatures, whether they are beetles in your backyard that are roaming around at night or small mammals. The principle is basically the same— a smooth-sided container sunk into the ground that, once something has fallen into, cannot scale the sides and escape.

Now, sand hoppers are little crustaceans vital to the running of the beach. They exist in their thousands and on a good beach you can actually turn over some weed and grab a handful of maybe thousands of the little hoppers and feel the odd sensation as one by one they fizz from between your fingers, leaving you grasping nothing but air. Sand hoppers are also called beach fleas.

But small and strange-looking though they may be, these creatures are vital to the recycling of dead material that gets washed up on the shore. Furthermore, they are also food for many other creatures, especially birds, which is why, on a desolate, windswept beach in the winter, you can often find wading birds, such as plovers, turnstones, purple sandpipers, and even smaller birds such as starlings, pipits, and horned larks, working their way along a strand line picking at these tiny little beach residents. If you don't believe me, just take an old jam jar with you next time you go to the beach (see opposite).

Grab a handful of sand hoppers and see how they hop! They don't jump like a grasshopper; instead they use their bodies as a spring.

YOU WILL NEED

> **large jam jar or bottom half of an old plastic soda bottle**
> **garden trowel**

2 Settle the jar within this hole so that the rim is flush with the surface. Cover with a piece of driftwood or seaweed.

3 Make a marker flag out of a stick and some weed so that you don't forget where you buried your trap.

1 As soon as you arrive at the beach find the strand line and dig a hole.

4 Come back the next day, remove your flag and seaweed or stone and remove the container from the hole.

5 You will be amazed at the numbers you can catch this way. As if you have chosen a sand hopper-friendly spot, your jar will be fizzing with these jumpy little crustaceans. You may have caught a few other strand line scroungers too, and maybe some ground beetles or even a large isopod or woodlouse. Have a close look at your sand hoppers— there is more than one kind!

Estuaries

In many ways an estuary is very similar to the soft shore habitat and many of their residents overlap and can be found in both places—but it is also unique in other ways. This habitat is a focal point for many other creatures and often they are found in incredible densities.

An estuary occurs when a river of fresh water meets the sea. What happens at this junction is that all those mineral-rich sediments that swirl around in the current of a river meet the sea head on, and stop. When the water stops moving, all the sediment sinks to the bottom. Exactly the same thing happens if you stop stirring your soup—the noodles disappear from sight and settle at the bottom! In an estuary, that sediment is known by the more familiar name of mud.

The river mouth at this point is a shallow bowl and so the mud collects in sheltered places, such as by the banks and shores, and these become tidal flats so loved by mud-dwelling microscopic plants and animals, which have a party on the rich, fertile estuary mud. These, in turn, feed a multitude of slightly bigger creatures, such as worms and mollusks, that are then stuffed into the mouths and beaks of fish and birds, and so on. Now that you know the basics of what makes estuaries such fabulous concentrations of wildlife, read on and find out more.

Common cockle

Fab facts

Each yard of estuary is a more productive habitat than a yard of forest, grassland, or farmland. San Francisco Bay, Chesapeake Bay, Puget Sound, Tampa Bay, and Boston Harbor are all examples of estuaries. You will often hear them called bays, lagoons, harbors, or inlets, rather than estuaries.

An aerial view of an estuary at low tide—a muddy vision of paradise.

Razorshells are more usually found on the sandier edges of some estuaries. They can also be seen on muddy beaches at low tide.

A clamworm—one of the secret inhabitants of many an estuary.

Flat fish, such as this plaice, enjoy the shallow waters of estuaries.

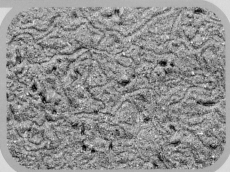

These are the holes of mud shrimp, a creature that is important food for many birds and fish in an estuary.

Mud lovers

One of my favorite ways to waste time is to pop down to my local estuary on a bright winter's day at low tide to watch the birds. Wherever there is mud, there will be birds probing, prodding, and skimming it for food—bird watching anywhere is so much more than just making a list of the different kinds you can see. It is also a particularly interesting thing to do on an estuary, as you will always be surprised at the numbers of species that can be seen at any one time.

Sanderlings can often be seen skittering up and down the mud of an estuary chasing the waves and hunting for tiny creatures disturbed by the water's movement.

The turnstone uses its short, blunt bill like a lever to flip over weed, stones, and other debris in the hunt for tiny creatures, such as worms and sand hoppers.

The heron is a fish stabber, watching and waiting for an unwary fish dinner to swim by.

Take it further

* Watch what the birds are up to. How do they feed? Some of the plovers have large eyes, suggesting good eyesight. Watch them hunt, they move in a series of dashes. Look, dash, peck, means they are spotting creatures moving in the mud.

* Others probe randomly, moving along and reaching into the mud. Little waders, such as dunlin, bob along like sewing machine needles, while whimbrels reach into the mud for larger, deeper-living beasts, such as worms and mollusks. Some, like the oystercatcher, are more violent, using their beaks to smash and grab.

* Avocets and many of the water fowl use a combination of techniques to sweep, scoop, and filter the goodies they are after out of the mud.

A typical estuary scene at low tide where there are more birds than you can count, all doing interesting things.

Nick's tricks

* To avoid seeing nothing but lots of little black dots way off in the distance, try to arrive around high tide. The best time is an hour or so on either side of high water. Check your local tide timetables for these. The birds will be focused on eating as much as they can before the incoming water means they can no longer reach the mud. High water squeezes the feeding birds closer to the shore, where they are much easier to see.

* Winter is the time when you will see many different species together as they form large winter feeding flocks. Most birds will be in their winter, non-breeding plumage, which is usually not nearly as interesting as their breeding dress. In the fall or spring, look for birds that are late or early in molting their feathers.

* In the winter, the Sun can be very low, so you really do not want to be squinting into it. It will make watching the birds both hard and unenjoyable. Get the Sun behind you, and what are just silhouettes from one side become full color images. Fantastic!

Grasping the razor

Razorclams are not fish at all but very long bivalve mollusks. They get their name because each of their valves looks a little like an old-fashioned "cut-throat" razor blade. Razorclams are rarely seen alive above the surface and even when we do get close, they retreat very, very fast in a downwards direction. You will be lucky if you manage to catch one when it is trying to escape from you from near the surface—they are incredibly quick swimmers!

Look in the right place. You need to be on a muddy or sandy beach and if you find the distinctive empty shells, there's a good chance that out at sea the live ones can be found. Then you need to wait until the lowest low tide of the month and walk along the lower shore as it is exposed by the retreating water.

Recognize the signs. While you are paddling along at the water's edge, you are looking for two things. One—a keyhole-shaped hole around half an inch long. This is the entrance to the razor's burrow and sometimes, if the sand is thin and muddy, this will look more like a shallow crater in the sand. Two—jets of water being squirted from the holes. This happens when a razorclam detects your footsteps and takes avoiding action. It retreats rapidly into its burrow, displacing a column of water as it travels.

That's about as close as most mortals would come to these fascinating mollusks, but to a curious naturalist, it simply isn't close enough. Catching them with your hands is possible, but you have to combine the stealth of a jaguar with the reflex speed of a bullet—see opposite. Even if you get hold of one before it vanishes, you still have a tug of war on your hands as these things are incredibly strong. They win more often than not, and you can do them damage if you get it wrong.

Sometimes you can find huge numbers of razorshells washed up by freak storms at sea.

1 Take your squirty plastic bottle to the water's edge and fill it with sea water.

2 Add three table spoonfuls of sea salt to the bottle. Give it a good shake so the salt dissolves and you are now ready to tackle the mysterious mollusk.

3 Walk gently while searching for your "key holes," and, when located, squirt a liberal amount of your super salty water down the hole. Either the shellfish decides the tide has come in and returns to the surface to feed or the salt water is an irritant and it tries to clear it from its burrow. Either way, within minutes the animal should head back to the surface. Sometimes just the top of its shell peeps out above the sand as it rises slowly like a subterranean elevator. In other cases, it shoots up like a missile.

Take it further

* Once you have sucessfully coaxed your razorclam to the surface, quickly grab it. Do not yank at it or you can injure the animal, but keep up a steady, gentle pressure and eventually you will find the razorclam will give up the tug of war and allow you to bring it to the surface.

* Once you have admired this living piston, place it back on the sand where you caught it. Watch the fascinating process as it pulls itself back down into the sand. The technique involves the razorclam pushing its long, muscular foot into the sand and then making the end swell up to act as an anchor. Slowly it drags its streamlined shell after it.

The tray of revelations

Just watch an estuary in the winter at low tide and it will be positively bustling with feathered activity. Wildfowl and waders feast on unseen myriad tiny creatures. It may not look like it, but the mud of an estuary is one of the richest and most productive ecosystems on the planet, up there with the tropical rainforests and coral reefs.

When a Black Brant goose scythes its bill through the surface of the slick mud, it is skimming for something worthwhile to eat. When a dunlin makes its way along like some maniacal nodding dog, it is not wasting its energy on nothing.

So to find out what makes these grey, uninviting plains of mud so interesting to the birds, you need to change your perspective. Put down your binoculars and pick up a tray and a trowel instead.

A Black Brant goose is a particularly keen devourer of laver spire shells—see step 4, opposite.

Fab fact

The small animals you reveal in the tray of revelations are some of the most numerous creatures on earth. They reach mind-boggling numbers of some 70,000 creatures for every square yard of the mud down to a depth of around 2 inches! That means that this quantity of good rich mud can contain nearly as much energy as around 13 candy bars! No wonder the wading birds have evolved all their strange beaks and behaviors to get at that rich resource.

1 Attach the spoon to the bamboo cane with a strip of duct tape. This will be helpful in scooping up the mud.

2 If you can find some fine mud at the edge of the estuary, try scooping up some of this stuff, being very careful not to get yourself stuck at the same time.

3 Take a tiny amount (just a couple of teaspoons' worth of mud), and stir it up in a cup of sea water. Then pour this weak muddy brew into the white tray and let it settle.

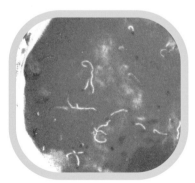

4 Watch as slowly, magic takes place. These are the trails left by the laver spire shells. At the end of each one is a little dark dot—the tiny snail's shell.

Take it further

* As you collect the mud, a spoonful at a time, you will find other miniscule monsters.

* Small shore crabs are very common, as are various mud shrimp. These live in shallow burrows under the mud surface, occasionally reaching out with their forelimbs to bulldoze around in the surface to extract goodies from the ooze. These active creatures are what many of the plovers and sandpipers are looking for.

* You may also catch a few of the surface-hunting worms. Clam worms can look a little like Chinese dancing dragons; a combination of their frill-like appendages, fast frantic movement, and the bright green color.

Shrimps

These glassy and rather beautiful crustaceans can be studied in a number of ways, but first things first—can you tell the different types apart from one another? The easiest way is to look at where you are catching them. They can hide in mud and sand or in oyster beds.

You can watch them go about their business by attracting them with bait or watching them with an underwater viewer (see pages 14 and 24), but to see them close up is to reveal their stunning translucent beauty and for this you need to dig out your observation tank again. Catch them with a bottle trap (see page 17)—a home-made mini lobster pot—or you can use a net.

When you catch a true shrimp, put it into your observation tank complete with its sand and sea water and watch what happens. Your shrimp will do its magic and vanish right before your eyes! Try to work out what movements the shrimp makes to help it bury itself from sight so quickly.

Take my advice

* Forget those flimsy, brightly colored nets that you see for sale at most seaside stores. They are next to useless and you may as well not bother buying them. Instead, invest in or make your own. Any net to be used on the shore needs to have a stout and robust frame and similarly strong netting.

* As with all nets, different ones are designed for different jobs but a good multipurpose one will have reasonably coarse netting and a weight, either lead or stone, sewn into the bottom of the pouch to help keep it open.

* The coarse netting is perfect for catching bigger creatures like shrimps and crabs as their legs can get tangled up in the finer ones, making them harder to extract, and you risk them losing limbs and getting damaged. This type of net is often sold at fishing stores for catching shrimps and crabs.

1 Traditional shrimping nets have a flat edge to them, as here, while crabbing nets are rounded.

2 In sandy or soft muddy areas, walk along in the shallow water, pushing the net in front of you. Skimming just under the surface is the best way to catch all kinds of creatures, as this ensures that anything that buries itself at the first sign of danger is caught.

Take it further

* If you are using a net in a rock pool, quickly bring it up under fringes of weed. This is the best way to catch the creatures living there as they have no choice but to swim down into your net.

* Or you can lie in ambush. Rest your net on the bottom and place some bait in its center and then you can quickly bring it to the surface when something interesting comes to investigate.

* For catching smaller, more delicate creatures, the little nets sold for use in aquariums are the best. They have stout wire frames, come in a range of sizes and are relatively cheap.

Cliffs

A cliff is something certain. It is a line on a map and a definite end to the confusion of the beach and the clear beginning to the land. I have included the cliff habitat in this book because it is very interesting to the naturalist for all sorts of reasons. It's land with a salt-sprayed, wind, and ocean-battered difference!

Where the ocean chews away at the land, the waves beat it to a pulp. Some of the waves are loaded with sand and stone. Cliffs are a history lesson as they throw open the story of the land to the present—and this is where fossils come in (see page 66).

The character of the cliffs depends on the rocks making them and the landscape. Soft, crumbly cliffs are unstable but provide a soil that is perfect for solitary bees and wasps to dig into. Or there are steep granite cliffs with their towers and turrets that make excellent nesting ledges for sea birds.

Our shore lines are far from stable and are always changing shape. The sea batters away at cliffs, wearing them down with a constant beating of water, air, and the grit and sand that each wave contains. Likewise, gales and storms do an often spectacular job of throwing up sandbars and shifting hundreds of tons of sand and pebbles here and there.

Try documenting this change. If you live near the coast or regularly visit one particular patch, try to choose a spot that you won't forget easily and use this as a position to take a photograph from. Every time you visit that same place, take another photo to use as a comparison. Over a period of time you will be shocked at the effects the power of the ocean has. Another comparison can be made if you scour old books or postcards for coastal scenes taken many years ago. It can be fun to try to find where they were taken and just how much the shape of the coast has changed over time.

Like icing on a cake, the white droppings of large numbers of sea birds here on these cliffs show that this is a popular spot for nesting.

Sea bird city—a murre colony at the height of the breeding season. It's never a dull place!

The lines in these cliffs tell of the fact that they were laid down in the past as layers of mud or sand at the bottom of the ocean.

Watch out!

Interesting though they may be, cliffs can also be dangerous places because they are always shifting. All it takes is for an unaware naturalist to jump around a little for a land slip to occur or for bits of the cliffs to fall off. So, for these reasons, do not climb or clamber on cliffs, stay away from edges and overhangs, and do not do anything that may cause them to collapse.

See sea birds

Because of the inherent dangers of climbing and scrabbling about on cliffs this is a real no-no, but there is a lot you can learn about birds just by looking at them and their habitat. So, first of all, take a long, hard look at the cliffs from a distance through a pair of binoculars. You will see that nothing other than a few climbing and clinging plants can actually live on the vertical bits—and that goes for the sea birds, as well. It may seem that they are hanging off the cliff face but they almost certainly will have found a little ledge to perch on. Patches of greenery and flowering plants are also a good sign that there is a horizontal root hold here.

On dark rock, look out for white stains that look as if a paint tin has been emptied down a cliff. These are the droppings of birds, so tend to point at the location of a frequently used ledge above, which may turn out to be a nest site. If you are looking at white chalk or limestone cliffs, you need to look for the green stain that occurs when bird droppings fertilize the surface enough for algae to grow.

All cliffs will provide nest sites for some birds. They may be smaller, more common birds, like sparrows and goldfinches, but you may also find warblers and pipits using the safety of grassy ledges and the occasional bravely rooted bush. Birds of prey like kestrels and peregrines can add a dramatic burst of energy to any coastal scene. What you see depends on where you are looking, but just remember you rarely see everything.

All nesting birds are attracted to the security that these locations bring. None more so than on very steep and tall stacks and island cliffs. These are not only in close proximity to the sea and therefore food, but they also make life very difficult for land predators such as rats, cats, foxes, and weasels to get to the birds.

If you make a trip to a sea bird colony, take your field guide, notebook, and a packed lunch, as you may want to stay for some time.

Just like in a human city, some birds love crowded ledges, others nest among boulders at the bottom of the cliffs, and some, like puffins, prefer the green lawns to be found on top of the cliffs.

Take my advice

When nesting sites on stacks and rocky islands occur, we get a sea bird city. These often huge colonies are best visited in early summer as you will get to see the early nesters, such as the cormorants, as well as some of the later birds. It is well worth any amount of traveling to get to see them, even if you have to convince your parents to do it. The experience of murres, razorbills, puffins, kittiwakes, and a cormorant all in the same field of view has got to be worth a trip, and it is also a great opportunity to brush up on your sea bird ID as, for the most part, many of these species remain far away from land, drifting the world's oceans.

Take it further

Once you have identified some of the birds you can see both in flight and settled, look around for other activities and behavior.

* What birds are in pairs?

* What happens when a solitary bird is met at the nest by another?

* Can you see any eggs? If so, what do they look like?

* Can you see large predatory gulls like greater black-backed gulls trying to steal chicks and unguarded eggs?

* In the water at the base of the cliffs, can you see birds fishing and diving, sometimes showing you a rare glimpse of them swimming below the surface?

* Can you see chicks being fed? And if so, what with?

Time travel

It is possible to time travel by doing nothing more than sitting on a boulder and staring up a cliff face. Any cliff that was laid down as deposits were nearly all at one time the bottom of seas or lakes and their layers were built up as sediment and silt drifted down and settled on the bottom. So from where you are sitting, the rocks you are looking at are millions of years old and if you whizz your eyes to the very top, the layers get younger and younger. They really are a time slice and if you know what you are looking for, you may well come across fossils; imprints of creatures long since past. Now, you may get lucky and find a smallish stone or rock complete with its own fossil, but more often than not they are embedded in the surface of rocks and boulders far too big to shift, let alone slip into your pocket!

It may be tempting to go get a hammer and chisel and start chipping away. But many sites are protected by law. You should never trespass on private property or enter sites without permission. And you should never collect or keep anything until you have checked all the laws for that area.

One way that you can start your own fossil collection is to make casts of them (see Take it further, opposite). By making a cast, you can have copies of your finest finds in your bedroom, leaving the real one where it had been for millions of years for other users of the beach to enjoy in passing. Pursue your fossil hunting by trying to identify what kind of fossils you have found.

Fossil hunting catches the imagination— you never know what you are going to find, or when.

Some examples of the wide variety of fossils that you might find when hunting: a hazel leaf (opposite), shell (left), and an ammonite (below).

Take it further

* To make a cast, you will need to take modeling clay and a shoe box to the beach. Beside your fossil find, knead the clay until it is very soft. Push it into the rock containing your fossil so it fills every crack and crevice. Slowly peel back the clay to reveal a good imprint. Put your imprint into the box to protect it and take it home.

* Once home, gently flatten your "fossil," being careful not to disturb the surface. Trim it with a kitchen knife to an even shape. Then use more modeling clay to build a "wall" an inch high around the "fossil."

* Now for the messy bit: mix some plaster of Paris powder with enough water to make a smooth liquid. It needs to just drip off the spoon. Quickly pour into the mold around your fossil cast. Jiggle a little so that any air bubbles are released.

* Wait for the plaster to set hard (at least 30 minutes) and then carefully peel away the modeling clay from the plaster. What you have is a perfect replica of your fossil and with an artistic hand you could paint it to resemble the original or you could be bold and make up your own color scheme that shows off your fossil to the best effect.

Sea watching

At low tide, as you stand with the waves lapping at your toes, behind you there is the wonderfully rich and diverse world of the intertidal zones that you have already explored. But in front of you, there is the final frontier of the coastal naturalist—the open ocean. Just a vast twinkling wilderness that is still surprisingly little understood and all you get from where you stand are small, frustrating glimpses. So how do you get to know the ocean itself? The ultimate is to become a diver or take up snorkeling. Both are specialist skills that are beyond the scope of this book. Other options include taking one of the many tours and boat trips that go on around the coast advertising whale, seal, or sea bird watching trips, or you can do what I spend many hours doing, and that is sitting on top of a good vantage point gazing out at the sea, an activity known by the most unsurprising title of "sea watching!"

The technique is simple. Find a sticky-out piece of land that juts into the ocean and sit on it! Not only do you get a height advantage, which means you can see farther and down into the water, but also headlands act as a focus for marine life. Just by staring out to sea you put yourself in the right place to see some of the most exciting creatures in the oceans.

Potentially you could get glimpses of a whale or dolphins and even the second biggest fish in the world, the basking shark. If you do not get lucky on the charismatic mega fauna, you will almost certainly get to watch sea birds. The best conditions are when the ocean is flat and calm.

Scan the ocean and you might just see the backs of porpoise or a dolphin gleaming in the sun. At a distance, identification can be tricky—look for the color and shape of the dorsal fin.

Get your hands on a pair of binoculars or even a telescope. Both are good investments for wildlife watching but never more useful than when you have a pod of bottle-nosed dolphins or a shark down the end of one! With a careful scanning, you will notice any disturbance to the smooth ocean surface caused by a shark fin or a dolphin or whale. Look for clues such as a shining flank catching the light or what looks like a wave breaking, or even heading in the opposite direction to the current. Watch the bows of boats for dolphins riding the pressure waves. Large "snow drift" flocks of sea birds such as gulls or terns often indicate fish near the surface and are also a good focal point for dolphins or harbor porpoise. Sitting on top of a cliff is actually more exciting than it sounds!

Smooth, glassy water conditions are best for sea watching as any disturbance to the surface from below will easily show up.

Take it further

At certain times of the year you can watch streams of birds migrating up and down our coasts and feeding frenzies as fish and other food get close to the surface. Rough times out at sea can often drive closer to land truly ocean-going species that cannot normally be seen from the shore.

Going further

This book was never meant to be anything but the very beginning of a journey—I see it as being the map, the compass, and a kick in the right direction. As you continue to explore various coastal habitats, you will begin to ask more questions and discover things that this book may not be able to answer. This is why this section exists—to give you a few more pointers in the right direction.

 Good reading

Marine Life of the North Atlantic (1994. Text and photography by Andrew J. Martinez and Richard Harlow, Marine Life, P.O. Box 335, Wenham MA 01984. ISBN 0-9640131-0-X).

Florida's Fabulous Seashells and Other Seashore Life (2001. By Winston Williams. 10th edition. World Publications, Tampa, Florida. ISBN 0-911977-05-8).

Southeastern and Caribbean Seashores (1988. By Eugene H. Kaplan. Peterson Field Guides, Houghton Mifflin Company, Boston. ISBN 0-395-31321-X).

A Field Guide to the Atlantic Seashore (1978. By K. Fosner. Peterson Field Guides, Houghton Mifflin Company, Boston).

Guide to Marine Invertebrates: Alaska to Baja California (1994. By Daniel W. Gotshall. Sea Challengers. Monterey, California. ISBN 0-930118-19-7).

Between Pacific Tides (1985. By E.F. Ricketts, J. Calvin, J.W. Hedgpeth. 5th edition revised by David W. Phillips. Stanford University Press, Berkeley, California).

Handy organizations

National Audubon Society:
700 Broadway, New York, New York. 10003-9562
One of the oldest US big conservation organizations with sanctuaries and nature centers throughout the country including many coastal reserves. Conducts annual Christmas Bird Count – www.audubon.org

The Ocean Conservancy: Washington DC and elsewhere

Marine Conservation Society:
Washington DC
Active primarily in political lobbying for national and international marine protection.

The Nature Conservancy:
Arlington, VA
Owns coastal reserves on both coasts. Primarily concerned with the protection of biodiversity.

U.S. Fish and Wildlife Service:
Interior Department, Washington DC
Operates the National Wildlife Refuge System, the most extensive reserve system for wildlife protection in every state. Activities vary greatly by location. Has many active coastal reserves.

Handy stuff – equipment supplies and other contacts

Memphis Net and Twine
Memphis, Tennessee
www.memphisnet.net

Carolina Biological Supply

Forestry Suppliers Inc.
www.forestry-suppliers.com

Index

Author's acknowledgments

> Big thanks to the energetic and hardworking team at HarperCollins who put this book together. Especially the tireless Helen Brocklehurst—how she holds everything together when it comes to building books, I don't know. But thankfully she does and she's good at it. And the same for Emma Callery, who as editor for this book has endured the frustrating half-finished manuscripts, bad grammar and spelling and, of course, the continual frustration of not being able to get hold of me on the phone! Thanks for not shouting at me and getting cross! Nikki English, the photographer, who has the patience of a saint and found the energy to continue wrangling animals and children both at the same time, AND managing to take great photographs; surely the definition of multi-tasking!

> The children—Aaron, Barney, George, Jack, Jed, Lucy, Martha, Megan, Millie, and Will—for all their patience with us and the props, cameras, and animals. I would especially like to thank Barney for reminding me what it was like to be a young naturalist.
> Gerard Bertrand for invaluable advice on this edition of the book.